Ephesus, The Ancient Capital City of Anatolia

Preface

Ephesus is a city that most of us have heard of but aren't especially familiar with. This book is a detailed account of what lies behind the city walls and what the history of the city looks like.

In this book, you will learn:

- All about the famous citizens and visitors of the ancient city
- What the Temple of Artemis was like, and why it was so important
- All about Alexander the Great and his connection to the city
- What did Mark Antony and Cleopatra do in Ephesus?
- How many different cultures inhabited the walls, and why they were defeated
- The legend of the Seven Sleepers

Table of Contents

Introduction

What do you think of when you hear someone mention the country of Turkey? Cool blue seas with golden beaches? Busy markets filled with exotic spices and fake handbags? Perhaps you imagine crowded streets with gnarled old men smoking bongs and talking about local politics. The fact is that you will see all of these things if you visit Turkey and so much more. There are sites in Turkey that mark some of the hardest-fought battles from modern wars, and there are places of such poignancy that they will make you shed a tear for the lives that were lost there.

But what about historical sites? Turkey is filled with places that are so historically important that they are visited by thousands of people every day. Istanbul is amazing and contains some of the most impressive architectural structures you will ever see. The Topkapi Castle is a must-see monument to the Ottoman Empire, and the Cappadocia Underground City will take your breath away. However, in this book, we are all about Ephesus, the vibrant former capital city that is a magnet for scholars and enthusiasts of Greek and Roman history. It provides them with a chance to walk along the same streets as some of the most famous people from those cultures and others. It is a hugely important place for Christians and other faiths, and it is such an eclectic mix of cultures.

This treasure trove for enthusiasts is waiting to tell you its story and relive its former glory. Are you ready for the visit? Then let's step back in time and see what lies in wait for us in the magnificent city of Ephesus. Enjoy.

Chapter 1:

The Ephesian Timeline

Ephesus is an important historical site featuring heavily in Pagan and Christian records. It has been influential since well before the birth of Christ and was then an important site connected to the Virgin Mary and St. Paul. It was one of the biggest settlements in the world and was home to some of the world's greatest thinkers.

Later in the book, there will be more details about the buildings, the people that populated them, and why there is so much interest in the site today. There will also be suggestions of ways to visit the site and what to expect from the area, but to whet your appetite; we will start the journey with a timeline of the city and a brief historical overview of Ephesus to whet.

Ephesus Timeline

The origins of the site are sketchy and are believed to date from 5000 - 3000 BC, but the details are limited.

We know there were settlers there, but little is known about them or how their civilization lived.

- **5000 - 3000 BC** – The first settlers are thought to have come from the Ionian region, which was situated in modern-day Turkey in an area known as Western Anatolia. There are records of their existence from 1150 BC, and they are believed to have traveled to Ephesus in the early part of the city's existence.

- **1100 BC** – The Ionians arrived in Ephesus and settled there. One of these settlers was reputedly Androclus, the legendary founder of Ephesus and the skilled hunter who was featured in many myths and tales from the era.

- **800 BC** – The first evidence of the invasion of Ephesus by the Cimmerian.

- **700 BC** – The Lydians capture Ephesus.

- **500 – 300 BC** – Recorded as the oldest place of settlements around Ephesus. Between 550 and 430 BC, the Temple of Artimus was constructed and was later included in the Seven Wonders of the Ancient World.

- **550 BC** – Aristarchus of Athens introduces democracy to Ephesus.

- **547 BC** – Anatolia is invaded and conquered by the Persians. Ephesus remains neutral.

- **356 BC** – The famed madman and arsonist Herostratus burned the Temple of Artemis on the same night that Alexander the Great was born.

- **334 BC** – Alexander the Great liberated all Greek cities and granted funds and privileges to the Ephesians to rebuild the temple that had been destroyed 22 years earlier.

- **330 BC** – The new Temple of Artemis was completed.

- **319 – 281 BC** – The leadership of Ephesus was changed multiple times, and the area was plagued with the Diadochean wars.

- **306 BC** – Lysimachus succeeds Alexander the Great and becomes the King of Thrace and renames Ephesus Arsineia in honor of his wife, the daughter of Ptolemy. The city is moved to a new site between two mountains for security reasons.

- **281 BC** – Following Lysimachus' death, Ephesus was taken by the Seleucid dynasty and made part of their empire.

- **133 BC** – The death of Attalus III leads to the bequest of Ephesus to the Roman Empire.
- **88 BC** – Ephesus welcomes the King of Pontus, leading to the death of 80,000 Romans during the bloody invasion.
- **84 BC** – Roman dictator and general hold trials of the Ephesians responsible for the slaughter of the Romans in 88 BC.
- **41 BC** – Mark Antony and Cleopatra enter Ephesus, where Cleopatra's sister is murdered by Antony, despite seeking sanctuary in a church.

After the Birth of Christ

- **23 AD** – A major earthquake hits the city, destroying much of the infrastructure. Reconstruction began backed by imperial help.
- **52 – 55 AD** – Ephesus is visited by former disciple Paul who gives daily talks in the school for over two years.
- **113 – 114 AD** – Roman emperor Trajan visits Ephesus as the first emperor of non–Italian origin. Some references say he was Iberian, while others claim he was of Hispanic blood with Italian lineage.

- **124 AD** – The first visit of Emperor Hadrian to Ephesus.
- **262 AD** – A major earthquake hits the region. The Temple of Artemis is destroyed by Goths.
- **431 AD** – The fourth ecumenical council is held in the city, and the members declare that Mary is officially the mother of God.
- **530 AD** – The first record of the legend of the Seven Sleepers of Ephesus.
- **550 AD** – Around this time, Justinian 1st, the emperor of Rome, built the great Basilica of St. John.
- **654/55** – Muslim Arabs lead the battle of the masts and attack Ephesus.
- **1300 AD** – The Turkish tribe retakes the area and declares it part of their empire.
- **1500 AD** – The rise of the Ottoman Empire includes the taking of Ephesus.
- **1863 – 74** – The British explorer and engineer J.T. Wood started excavations in Ephesus.
- **1904** – The British Museum sends a team of archaeologists to Ephesus.

- **1995** – Austrian archaeologists begin to collaborate with Turkish experts to find more information.
- **2009** – Over 170 scientists from 11 countries worked with local teams to complete five months of excavations, which uncovered some of the most historically important relics from the site.

Today the site is incredibly popular with tourists and brings in high revenue with over two million visitors per year, and this puts pressure on the team still working to uncover even more artifacts. The site is iconic, and it can be difficult to marry the pressures of tourism and marketing with the dedicated work of goal-orientated research, but the team does a fabulous job.

The site has been subject to archaeological interest for 130 years and has far exceeded the time originally allotted for its excavation. In 1893 it was the subject of plans submitted to the Ministry of Culture that suggested the whole site could be uncovered in a mere five years. Luckily for us, that work is still going on today.

A Broad Overview of Life in the City of Ephesus

There have been multiple societies that have lived in Ephesus and who had differing experiences, just like the rest of society. The difference with Ephesus is that it is a mirror of the area and highlights the very best of society during each period. It is also a classic example of how times change, and even the most influential and important cities can lose their place in history and become relics of the past.

The Amazons

Legend has it that Ephesus was founded by a race of "superwomen" known as Amazons, and this theory is strengthened by the discovery of a "labrys," the Greek symbol of female strength being found there and on the island of Knossos Crete, which indicated the presence of strong women. This female influence was also thought to have added kudos to the building of the Temple of Artemis, another female deity that was very powerful in Greek mythology.

The Greek Ephesus

The city was founded for the second time by the Ionian leader Androclus who gathered the migrating population of Ionia and settled them in Ephesus. The city was part of a devastating invasion in 700 BC, and leadership was taken by the Cimmerian hordes. Under the rule of the Lydian kings, the city began to prosper and found its place in the region as a center of learning and excellence, where women were considered equal and enjoyed the same benefits as their male counterparts.

There were female artists, scholars, and teachers. Female artists from the time painted bright, vibrant works of art, and one of them, Timarete, is renowned for her iconic work which depicts the city at night and the leader Artemis strolling through brightly lit streets with ornate oil lamps lighting his way. Not many cities in 500 BC had the same facilities or sense of population and a high level of living for even the poorest citizens.

King Croesus of Lydia became the city's new leader in 585 BC and brought heightened wealth and construction to Ephesus, along with his vision for the city's growth. His conquest meant that Greek rule was coming to an end, and the area became a Persian acquisition, but Ephesus continued in its role as a crucial port, and the fight for rulership didn't change that fact. The Ionian states rebelled against their Persian invaders, but Ephesus was allowed to remain neutral due to the importance of its trading status.

Hellenistic Ephesus

The Persians ruled for centuries until the city was liberated by Alexander the Great in 334 BC when he re-entered his home city after traveling and conquering other lands. When his home city revealed the ruins of the mighty Temple of Artemis, Alexander the Great offered the Ephesians funds to rebuild, but they were unwilling to take them, believing it would leave the city in debt to the great leader. When Alexander was succeeded by his general Lysimachus, it was deemed the right time to begin the reconstruction of the temple and development of the city following the destruction the Persians had inflicted.

Lysimachus's extensive plans involved moving the city between two mountains approximately 2 miles south of the original site. He constructed a new harbor and created strong defensive walls to keep the new site safe. When he changed the city's name to Arsineia in honor of his wife, it was too much for some of the residents who refused to leave the original city and move to the revamped version. Lysimachus waited until the night of a great storm when he ordered his soldiers to block up the original city's sewage system. This forced the residents to leave their sewage-infested homes and join the other citizens at the new site.

Following the death of Lysimachus, the city was renamed Ephesus once more and was re-established as an important port and became the hub of trading once more.

Roman Ephesus

In 129 BC, the end of the Hellenic era was in sight, and the Hellenistic period was ending. The last Hellenic king left the city of Ephesus to the Roman dynasty in his will. He recognized that the only way to keep any of his kingdoms intact and free from invasion by the mighty Romans was to bequeath them in their entirety to the powerful Roman forces.

The Roman government of the time immediately set about imposing heavy taxes, and the Ephesians weren't happy. They formed together to lead a rebellion against their leaders known as the Rebellion of Mithradates, a prominent Greek ruler who was one of the most effective and determined opponents the Romans were facing at the time. During the 57-year rebellion, there was a fateful day that saw the massacre of all Latin speakers in the area, with over 80,000 Romans being killed in just one day. Mithridates had overseen the infamous Asiatic Vespers massacre, which left Ephesus and the surrounding cities devastated and suffering huge losses.

Despite its bloody and violent history, Ephesus managed to regain peace and its important place in society. Even when an earthquake devastated the city in 17 AD, it recovered and was once more a commercial center of excellence. Its reputation for scholastic excellence and learning led to the construction of the impressive Celsus Library, which became the second school of philosophy in the Aegean area. This made the Aegean a natural place to visit for the great thinkers of the world, and it enjoyed a stream of gifted scholars and philosophers through the ages.

Following the death of Jesus, Ephesus became a natural meeting place for early Christians. Saint Pau was a resident, as was Mary, the mother of Jesus, who retired to the city with her beloved companion Saint John. Some of the many relics and artifacts suggest the city was a religious haven for these early visitors and became a symbol of faith for them, including the house of Mary and John's tomb following his death. There was also the Cave of the Seven Sleepers, which was reputedly a place where Christians were discovered. This tale will be described in more detail later in the book.

The Decline of Ephesus

While the city was a Christian stronghold, it also kept its pagan and pre-Christian communities where the different religious communities lived in harmony. This changed in 379 AD when the emperor Theodosius took control of the region. Christianity had become the dominant religion, and the emperor was an ardent follower of the faith. He issued a set of decrees that all pagan temples and schools should be closed, and women should be demoted to second-class citizenship. They were no longer allowed to teach men in the arts or to work independently in any of the areas they did before.

The Temple of Artemis was destroyed by a Christian mob, the Goths, and the once brightly lit streets were plunged into darkness. Decay and darkness fell upon the city, and even the Christian residents of Ephesus were left forgotten and in ruins. All they had to look forward to was being the Light of the World promised by their new God, Jesus Christ.

Chapter 2:

Famous People of Ephesus

Ephesus has had a long and colorful history, with many leaders and religions dictating how the citizens lived. In some eras, women were celebrated, and multiple religions existed in peace, whereas in other eras, there was suppression and bias that angered the citizens and made them revolt. Some of the more celebrated visitors and residents are also part of the fascinating past of Ephesus and provide an insight into why it was, and remains, one of the most amazing places to visit ever.

The Virgin Mary

After the ascension of Christ, Mary lived for three years on Mount Zion and another three years in Bethany before she went to Ephesus to join her beloved friend John, a former disciple of Jesus. Before she arrived, he had already built the house for Mary and chose caves and rocks outside of the city to make her home. There were several Christian families in the area, and the environment was safe and perfect for the families that chose to seek refuge.

The families had houses built into the caves and rocks to form a small village-like atmosphere, with each home being within a fifteen-minute distance from their neighbors. Most of the dwellings were similar to hermits' homes and formed by the natural materials available, but Mary's home was the only stone-built dwelling in the area. The view from the back of her house was spectacular and afforded a view of Ephesus and the sea with a clear view of the many islands of the area. Her house was simple but effective and divided into small areas where she could sit beside the fire and cook her simple fare. She lived with a maidservant who would travel to local agoras to bring food for her mistress and the visitors that would sometimes arrive and stay.

You can visit Mary's house in the present ruins of Ephesus and gain a feel of the tranquility and peace she must have felt as she lived out her life in the Christian enclave that was her final resting place.

The Apostle Paul

Probably the most influential and persuasive Apostle of them all, Paul is intrinsically connected to Ephesus and the first Christian Church to be built there. But he did have his detractors and was booed in the early days of preaching to the Ephesians. Eventually, he stayed in Ephesus for years, and it is thought to be the place where he wrote his influential letters to the Corinthians and the Ephesians. During his lifetime, Paul visited Ephesus three times on his prolific missionary travels and was accompanied by his friends and fellow believers Priscilla and Aquila.

St. John

We have already discussed the first Christian community founded by the disciple of Jesus, who was known as the "disciple of thunder," and how important he was to Mary. When the Apostle Paul was killed by decapitation outside the walls of Rome, John became the leader of the Ephesian church and made it his mission to spread the word. He was joined on his mission by St. Paul, and the pair traveled to Asia Minor to convert the inhabitants to Christianity.

St. John was almost assassinated twice during his travels. The first attempt was poison added to his drink, which materialized into a physical snake and left the glass before he could take a drink. A miracle indeed. The second attempt was during his time of exile on the island of St. Patmos when the same method failed to kill him again. He returned to Ephesus and wrote his gospel in 95 AD before he died peacefully and was buried in the city's graveyard.

Heraclitus of Ephesus

One of the most famous sons of Ephesus was Heraclitus. A pre-Socratic philosopher who was self-educated and was unaffected by other philosophical schools or thoughts as they had yet to reach the city of Ephesus. Heraclites was described as a somber man with exemplary deep thinking and a unique insight into the importance of the duality of the universe and the constant change of elements and the primordial existence.

Contributions of the Philosopher Heraclitus

Fire as Part of the Soul

As an element, fire has always been attributed to the existence of life, but Heraclites took the thought process a step further. He considered fire as the central element that never ceased to burn and how it fueled the movement of the rest of the universe. His teachings showed fire as the physical and spiritual element that linked us all to the universe and the continuous movement of life.

Mobility Is the Basic Source of Existence

Heraclitus was a firm believer that inertia meant the universe would cease to be, and he believed that nothing was inert and the only way the world worked was with constant movement. He is credited with the phrase "nobody bathes in the same river twice," illustrating how nature is constantly changing and becoming more evolved. He believed in the flow of all parts that gave the universe arbitrariness to its actions but also illustrated the constant flow of energy.

The Principle of Causality

Everything that happens has a cause, yet nothing is the cause. Heraclitus was convinced that the initial cause of every action and natural phenomenon lay in one place. He named this place God, and believed that the ultimate journey of retrospection would always finish at the same point, a theological conclusion that led to the ultimate power of God and his creation of the universe.

Strabo

The Greek geographer was an important part of the history of Ephesus as he documented the area around the city and how the infrastructure worked. His book

"Geographica" is considered a detailed and informative work that has become a standard reference for the time. His description of Alexandria describes a city of lights and amazing thoroughfares wide enough for chariots to pass on either side.

Strabo wasn't just a geographer; he also had detailed theories about how lands and mountains were formed in the past. He studied the presence of seashells and other fossils to determine the source of water that formed the rivers of the area, and his books are still important reference points for modern geologists today.

Artemidorus of Ephesus is also a famous geographer who was born in Ephesus and was a source of reference for Strabo. He created a papyrus that was a detailed yet incomplete map of the area of Ephesus and the surrounding environs, which is a subject of contention among historians. Some believe it is genuine, while others have declared it as fake. Despite the misgivings, the papyrus was sold for over $3 million to Turin's Banco di San Paolo.

Rufus of Ephesus

A gifted physician, Rufus was born in the city in 70 AD and was an influential author who favored treating the elderly and slaves. His treaties and dietetics covered many subjects which are still relevant today. He was a prolific author, and some of his works have survived but the majority hasn't. He was a socially conscious physician who wrote about areas that were often neglected at the time.

His work includes:

- **On Satyriasis and Gonorrhea** - A book about hyper-sexuality and sexually transmitted diseases that was groundbreaking at the time.

- **Medical Questions** – Another groundbreaking book that helped other medical experts find out more about their patients by asking the right questions.

- **For Laypeople** – An antithesis of the book Medical Questions, which helped non–medical laypeople understand exactly what their doctors were telling them.

- **On Gout** – A book about the causes of gout and how it affects the body.

- **Case Histories** – Another informative text dedicated to cataloging medical cases and how symptoms and signs could tell you what ails you without having to see a doctor. A kind of Google medicine for the ancient world.

- **The Names and Parts of the Human Body** – A textbook for people interested in how the body works and how to use the correct medical terms for parts and organs.

- **Diet for the Elderly** – Rufus was one of the first physicians to address how the body changes and why diet should be altered to suit older palates and needs. He highlighted the need for more nutrition and vitamins and where these could be found.

- **The Treatment of Infertile Women** – Another groundbreaking text that helped these women rather than considering their condition untreatable.

Some of his lost works were just as impressive and have been mentioned in texts from other authors and sources.

Popes in Ephesus

Ephesus has always been an important part of the Christian faith ever since the house of Mary was declared as one of the fundamental parts of Christianity.

The Catholic Church has assumed financial and spiritual responsibility for the house of Mary, and it is considered a Christian Pilgrim Place of Hope. The last Pope to visit was Benedict XVI. Paul VI was the first pope to leave Italy and conduct pilgrimages across six continents on the most comprehensive papal pilgrimage ever. He visited Ephesus in July 1967 and began a tradition of pilgrimage that was taken up by his successor John Paul II when he returned to Ephesus in 1979.

The visit of Benedict in 2006 was the last visit of a pope to the region and was memorable as it was a direct attempt to mend bridges between Christians and Muslims. His four-day trip was centered on his visit to Ephesus, where he conducted mass at Mary's house. Security issues meant that only 250 people were allowed to directly attend the open-air service, but the mass was televised across the world.

Benedict started his address by using kind words to describe the Turkish nation, and he began his speech in Turkish and waved a huge Turkish flag. He is thought to have united the two faiths by reminding them that the mother of Christ is the most referred-to woman in the Koran and that both faiths consider the Ephesian site a place of worship.

Marc Anthony and Cleopatra

Perhaps the most celebrated lovers of ancient times, Antony and Cleopatra, never actually lived in Ephesus, but they may have met there when her father, Ptolemy XII, visited to form an alliance with the forces of Caesar. Cleopatra's sister was exiled to the city later when she spread rumors that Antony was plotting against Cleopatra and was eventually killed on the steps of the Tempe of Artemis by soldiers who were loyal to Antony.

Antony was fascinated by Hellenistic culture and was an admirer of Alexander the Great, a renowned son of Ephesus. As he began his tour of the newly acquired Roman Eastern Empires, he took advantage of the vast cultural distractions the area provided. When he entered the city of Ephesus, he was greeted by the spectacular sight of a procession of people dressed as satyrs and priestesses from the age of Bacchus, the God of wine and revelry. He was awarded the title of "Dionysus, the giver of joy," which was the first time he had been publicly acknowledged with the Greek title. This meant so much to him that Ephesus immediately became one of his favored cities.

When Antony moved on to Tarsus, he contracted the Queen of Egypt, Cleopatra, and asked her to join him on his tour. She understood that reconnecting with the Romans would help her political and social status, so she immediately made plans to join Antony in Tarsus. Knowing how to make a spectacular entrance Cleopatra played on his love of Greek culture and arrived in the port dressed as Aphrodite, the goddess of love. She reclined under a golden canopy as musicians played and was attended to by handmaidens dressed as sea nymphs and young men in the image of Eros. They wafted perfume across the water to engage the crowds that lined the port and to mesmerize Antony as he watched the whole amazing spectacle.

The Roman Antony was abandoned as his attendees rushed to line the banks of the river, and he was left speechless and off guard. When Cleopatra landed, he tried to take charge of the situation by inviting her to a feast, but she knew the power of being in control was too important to relinquish, so she reciprocated and asked Antony to join her in a banquet that had already been prepared. He accepted and arrived to find a dining area festooned with expensive carpets and cloths decorated with gems and precious metals. Large couches were arranged to seat Antony and his entourage, and Cleopatra told Antony they were her gift to him. Totally dumbstruck, Antony tried to compete with the Queen but soon realized that her domination was just a taste of things to come.

Throughout the ages, many have passed through the city of Ephesus, and their influence can be seen in the relics and artifacts still there. The most important visitors in modern times are tourists, and they bring the revenue that ensures the mighty city will always have a place in history and that any further discoveries will have a place where they can be displayed.

Chapter 3:

The Terrace Houses of Ephesus

The terrace houses of Ephesus are also known as the "houses of the rich," and were built in Roman times to house wealthy residents of the city. The six houses that have survived excavations are situated close to the grand Library of Celsus and have only been available for public viewing recently. The buildings are covered by a large glass dome to keep them safe and weather-proof, but which gives the whole area a spooky, silent feel, unlike how they would have sounded back in the 1st century AD when they were occupied.

The terrace houses of Ephesus are constructed around a spacious and light courtyard and are built on four levels. Each entrance is framed by a vaulted wall and leads through to stunning, spacious reception rooms tastefully decorated with works of art and hand-painted murals and frescoes. These houses were excavated in the 1980s and 90s and gave a greater understanding of how the wealthy citizens of Ephesus lived.

All the houses had modern conveniences, including underfloor heating, latrines, and clean water, which weren't always available to less wealthy citizens. The rooms were lavishly furnished and contained scenes of gladiatorial combat, caricatures, depictions of the gods, and even love letters to each other. Terrace House 2 has a decorative and detailed frieze depicting a famous battle from 117 AD and featuring the emperor Trajan. The majority of the houses were paved with mosaic floors made from simple black and white tiles, which formed patterns on the floor.

The Importance of the Dining Room

The most important room in the house was the dining room, where the occupants would entertain their guests. The room would be dominated by a large table with ornate legs made from marble and bronze, and the guests would seat themselves on elaborate benches while they ate and drank. Music would be played in the background, and musicians would play the flute and lyre to soothe the soul.

A Typical Shopping List of the Time

There is an example of a list of foods that would be purchased regularly on display at the terrace houses that includes:

- Hazel nuts
- Small figs
- Barley
- Cheese
- Onions

The lists weren't filled with very exotic or inspired foods because of one important reason - the Romans didn't really like to cook their own food. Considering that they loved to eat and entertain, their kitchens were remarkably small, but there was a reason for this. Ephesus had amazing shops and markets known as agoras where they could purchase ready-cooked food for their feasts. Why would they choose to have lavish kitchens and servants to cook for them when they could visit the ancient version of takeaway UberEATS and choose from a selection of dishes from around the world?

Remember that Ephesus was a hub of activity and trading, so ships from across the globe would stop and trade their wares so the food available would have been some of the best in the world. During the day, the men of the household would leave to work in the agoras or the bathhouses, while some would choose to work in the vineyards or olive groves to produce quality olive oil that was sold across the world. The females would stay home and work with textiles or teach children, as most education was home-based.

When the menfolk arrived home, it was time for the family to eat, and they would have simple fare like bread and cold meat with cheese and olives, but when the family entertained, it was time to show their guests what a good time looked like. Wild boar and beef would be served with lavish side dishes and copious amounts of wine. Romans loved to show off with lavish meals that would last for hours and sometimes even days.

Interesting fact: Marc Antony, a famous visitor to Ephesus, was also known for his vast appetite, and his slaves and servants would always prepare a meal suitable for over twenty people even when there were no plans for guests. They knew that on certain days he would be capable of eating and drinking such amounts and couldn't run the risk of underfeeding the gluttonous Roman.

The Commercial Agora

Situated near the Celsus Library, the commercial agora was the hub of the city and an important part of social interactions. It is no coincidence that it was situated close to the terraced houses of the Romans, as they would have been some of the more prolific customers in the agora. The Roman agora was built on the same site as the Hellenistic agora but was twice the size.

Imagine the scene, a packed courtyard measuring 110m squares with shops on either side. A covered walkway was provided for pedestrians, and a large sundial and water clock were in the center of the whole agora. The water clock was designed to drain away every twenty minutes so that any debaters would have the same amount of time to speak. In one corner of the agora was a busy slave trade market with crowds of people bidding to buy servants from Africa and across the continent to join their households.

Languages from across the globe could be heard, and people of all colors and races would be found chatting and swapping tales in the busy courtyard and the shops. Smells of spices and cooking would fill the air, and traders would be shouting to promote their wares. Elite Roman citizens would be found mixing with less privileged citizens, and the whole atmosphere would be lively and social, with the odd scuffle breaking out. Some of the rectangular rooms allocated for shopkeepers would sometimes be used as political meeting places or makeshift courtrooms to try petty criminals. Overall, the agora may have been the smaller of the two in Ephesus, but it was still a diverse and entertaining place to visit. The granite columns that supported the huge structure could have told amazing tales if they could talk. The excavation of the agora uncovered an inscription on the wall of the agora dedicated to the market supervisor that read:

"The people of Ephesus express their gratitude to agronomy, Eutuches, son of Menecrates, for having pre-empted a rise in the price of bread."

This inscription highlights the fact that even then, in ancient times, people were grateful for the simpler things in life and that bread was just as important then as it is now. They may have been part of a thriving society that was the hub of the area, but they all shared a commonality, they were all citizens of Ephesus.

Chapter 4:

The Temple of Artemis

Ephesus is the site of the remains of the famous Temple of Artemis, but the original structure was thought to have originated in 700 BC and was built by the Amazons. It was a bronze-age piece of land dedicated to the mighty goddess and had a small temple dedicated to Callimachus. It was destroyed in a flood, and the reconstruction was begun around 550 BC by the Lydian King Croesus and took ten years to complete. It is believed to be the first Greek structure built of marble, and the structure was surrounded by 36 impressive columns that were highly decorated and contained impressive friezes and artwork.

The Temple became an important attraction, and its visitors included kings, merchants, and dignitaries who would bring gifts for the goddess in the form of gems and precious metals. The Temple was also a place for refuge as the goddess was a patron of the persecuted and offered sanctuary to those fleeing punishment. The

Temple was a social area that would be packed with visitors and worshipers throughout the day and night, and this led to some of the more solemn and traditional citizens of the city rallying against its civil use. They believed the Temple lost some of its relevance to the spiritual god when everyone was granted access and would have preferred the Temple to be more sacred.

The destruction of the Temple in 356 BC is highly documented as being the work of the mad arsonist Herostratus who was credited with burning down the Temple on the night of the birth of Alexander the Great. However, some scholars believe that other people must have been involved in the arson because they would have needed to gain access to the wooden roof framing to start the blaze. Modern scholars have questioned if the arson could have been carried out by just one man and have suggested that a whole corps of guards and custodians would have to have been involved. They believe that the Temple's administration could have been involved because there were signs that the foundations were sinking; yet they couldn't justify resiting the Temple because of religious constraints.

Construction of the third version of the Temple began in 323 BC and took decades to complete. It was larger than the others and measured 137 m by 69 m, with impressive columns gilded with gold and silver. There were multiple altars and areas dedicated to the goddess and her powers, while other areas were dedicated to the Amazons and other religious influences from Ephesus' history. In 286 AD, Christianity was becoming more popular, and the followers of Christ and his teachings were a brutal lot who were intent on removing any churches, temples, and other places of worship that were dedicated to non-Christian deities. The Goths were a particularly effective race of Germanic people who featured heavily in the collapse of the Western Roman Empire, and they are accredited with the sacking of the former Temple of Artemis, which had been rechristened as the Temple of Diana under Roman rule.

It is believed that stones and columns from the Temple were used to construct other buildings in Ephesus and that some of the remains were used to build the Hagia Sophia in Istanbul. These claims are unsubstantiated but do make the story more mystical.

Numerous shrines and temples were built honoring Artemis, but the Temple of Artemis at Ephesus was unique. Ephesians refused to acknowledge her connections to Greece and believed she was connected to them in a personal way. When the Persians began to rule in Ephesus, they dealt with the Temple respectfully but did remove some important artifacts and moved them to Sardis, where another Artemis temple lay. They infiltrated the "Ephesian cult of Artemis" by importing Persian teachers and priests to join the locals, and this was inexcusable. There is evidence that the Persians helped with restoration, but native historians played down their part and made it seem like they resisted the restoration.

Ephesian Artemis

In traditional Greek mythology, Artemis was the sister of Apollo and the proclaimed virgin goddess of the hunt. She is pictured with flowing robes and golden hair and is often accompanied by animals like deer and horses. She is a fair maiden with a horde of attendants made up of nymphs and other creatures from the forests. She roams freely, and despite being the goddess of childbirth, she remains unsullied and chaste. She is willful and brave and is often depicted driving a golden chariot through forests and across the skies.

The Ephesian Artemis is very different. She is depicted with a more Egyptian and archaic form, with a human head and bust that continues down as a square, tapering, pillar-like form, while her legs and feet are bound by a highly decorated taper. Her upper half is covered with multiple breasts, symbolizing her connection to fertility. In a 16th-century villa in Italy famed for its fountains, there is an impressive depiction of the Ephesian Artemis with water spouting from her multiple bosoms. Some experts believe that the oval objects that cover her chest aren't meant to be breasts but are merely decorative, but that would have made her less threatening to Christian beliefs.

The arm of the Ephesian Artemis is also featured as a snake or serpent with its tail resting in its mouth. Some statues show this as a staff, while other interpretations attach the serpent to her body. The Christians who sought to destroy the Ephesian Artemis and all her temple relics used these "demonic" signs to encourage her demonization and remove her from Ephesus. The Christian approach was successful, and the Temple was razed. It would seem that there would be no fourth version, as Christians had no place in their worship of pagan idols like the Ephesian Artemis.

The Seven Wonders of the Ancient World

The origin of the list of preeminent buildings and sculptures that formed the original Wonders of the World isn't confirmed but is thought to have been compiled by the 200 BC writer, the Antipater of Sidon, but could also have been a famous mathematician of the time. The writer may not be significant, but the list is. It is a comprehensive list of amazing achievements, including the following phenomenon:

The Great Pyramids of Giza

The three pyramids were originally built to house the remains of three kings of Egypt, Khufu, Khafre, and Menkaure, and they were situated at Giza. The pyramid of Khufu is the most impressive and colossal building that has ever been built on Earth. It is made from over 2.3 million blocks of stone. The pyramid graves were robbed, and the insides of the pyramids were stripped completely when they were discovered, but the layout of the pyramids is still impressive and give an insight into the opulence and wealth of the era. The Great Pyramid is the only remaining structure from the list to still exist today.

The Hanging Gardens of Babylon

There is little information regarding the gardens, but they are thought to have been placed close to the Royal Palace in Babylon. Some experts believe they were rooftop gardens that inspired the title and that they were constructed in the 8th century BC. Some experts believe that the gardens were built on sloping hills, which gave the impression that they were suspended.

The Statue of Zeus at Olympia

The 12m high statue was built from cedarwood and coated with elaborate ebony and gold plating. The Symbol of Nike was placed on his right hand to represent victory, while an eagle sat on his left hand to highlight the majesty of the god. The statue was placed in the Temple of Zeus in 430 BC but only lasted for four years as the whole Temple was destroyed in 426 BC. It is thought that the statue was destroyed along with the Temple, but some text from the era suggests it was transported to Constantinople, where it perished in a fire 50 years later. There are no accurate replicas or copies today.

The Mausoleum of Halicarnassus

A monument was built for the tomb of Mausolus by his sister and widow, Artemisia II. The tomb was a huge structure topped with a chariot atop a pyramid. It was designed by four separate architects who each designed one side of the tomb. It was built in the 4th century BC but was destroyed by an earthquake. All that remains today are ruins.

The Colossus of Rhodes

The mighty bronze statue of the sun god Helios was constructed in the harbor of Rhodes to celebrate the victory siege of Demetrius in the 4th century BC. It was constructed of bronze and weighed down with stones, and stood 32 meters high. The statue took 12 years to build and was toppled by an earthquake in 226 BC. The statue remained in the bay until 654 AD when raiding Arabian forces broke the statue into pieces and sold it for scrap.

The Lighthouse of Alexandria

Built around 280 BC, this lighthouse is an engineering triumph and the most famous lighthouse in antiquity. It was the archetype for future lighthouses and was the second-greatest man-made structure of the time. Only the Great Pyramids would have topped its height as it towered 110 m over the port of Alexandria and warned ships of rocks and other hazards. The beacon was added to the list of Wonders in the 6th century AD and replaced the Walls of Babylon. The lighthouse was still standing in the 12th century AD but was replaced by a mosque in the 14th Century when its ruins were used to complete other buildings.

It is truly humbling to consider what these amazing structures looked like and the superhuman efforts it took to build them. The ancient world was a time when men and women were discovering engineering and using it to create these fantastic structures. There would have been a huge human cost, and slaves would have been sacrificed in the name of progress, but without their efforts, we would all still be living in caves! While the majority of these wonders are gone now, their splendor and magnificence can still be appreciated from texts and reconstructions that have been painstakingly compiled by historians.

Chapter 5:

The Myths of Ephesus

Despite the long history of Ephesus, there are very few myths and legends attached to the city. Maybe the rich history and real-life happenings were so compelling and interesting that they superseded the need for myths. These are the most famous myths attached to Ephesus.

Amazons

The tribe of fearsome women who are believed to be the first occupants of Ephesus was the early forerunners of girl power. They lived in female-only communities and slept with men just once a year. They would choose their mate and sleep with them simply to proliferate their race. If the union produced a male child, it would be left with its father to raise, and any female children would be accepted into the tribe.

The origin of the name Amazons is thought to have originated from the word "Mazons," which translates to "breasts" and suggests that the Amazon warriors would remove one breast to make their armor more effective and help them to use their weapons with ease. Other experts believe that the prefix was added to the word to emphasize women who fought like men. Depictions of Amazons with two breasts support this theory.

The Amazons featured in a Greek legend that involved Zeus and his affair with a human woman resulting in the birth of a son called Hercules. Zeus's wife Hera was jealous of this progeny and set 12 tasks for Hercules to complete believing he would be dead at the end of his quest. One of the missions was to retrieve the golden belt of the Amazon Queen Hippolyte, which she believed would be impossible. Hercules and his friend Theseus entered the land of the Amazons and were welcomed warmly by the Queen. She offered the belt as a gift, which enraged Hera so much that she disguised herself as an Amazon, and caused massive disruption in the land of the Amazons. The result was the death of Hippolyte and the kidnapping of her sister by Theseus. He took his hostage back to Athens and kept her imprisoned. The remaining Amazons were outraged and traveled to Athens to free their captured comrade, which led them to Ephesus and the establishment of the city.

Many reliefs of Amazon women were found in the ruins of Ephesus and were completed by different artists. These reliefs can be seen at the Ephesus Museum in Selcuk near the official ruins.

The Origins Myth of Ephesus

The King of Athens, Codros, ruled in 1089 BC, and his son was Androcles, who was tasked with finding a new settlement for his people. He was leading a migration convoy to escape the Dor troops who were invading Greece and forcing the move. He consulted an oracle of Apollo to guide him to the new settlement and how to keep his people safe. The oracle told him that the location of the new settlement would be revealed by the appearance of a fish and a boar.

Just days later, Androcles was sitting by a river and frying a fish in a pan when the fish suddenly jumped from the fire and fell into a nearby bush. The flying fish startled a boar that was hiding in the bush, and it took flight immediately. Androcles followed the boar and hunted it down, killing it with an arrow. When the boar fell, Androcles remembered the oracle and what it had told him. He established the city of Ephesus in the very spot where the boar had fallen and led his people to safety. When Androcles fell in battle, the people of Ephesus built a huge mausoleum to their founder to commemorate the event.

The Seven Sleepers

The battle between pagans and Christians is one that raged for centuries following the death of Christ. There are epic tales of persecution and miracles throughout history, which tell of the bravery and resolution that many Christians have shown in the name of God. There are multiple cave-based legends, especially in Eastern and Western cultures and religions, because hermits often believed they were places of spiritual enlightenment and inspiration. Many shamans believed that caves were the portals to the supernatural world and would open up to welcome them into the realms of magic. This tale is similar as the cave serves as a haven for the occupants and keeps them safe from their persecutors.

The cave of the seven sleepers is situated on the slopes of Mount Pion, which is near the city of Ephesus. The legend of the cave was first recorded by a Greek scholar in the 10th century AD and tells the tale of

Christians who were steadfast in their beliefs during pagan times.

Decius was a pagan emperor who ruled in Ephesus between 249 and 251 AD, and he was steadfast in his quest to rid the city of Christians. Seven noblemen were leading Christians of the era and were summoned by the emperor to abandon their beliefs and return to pagan ways. The emperor realized that if he could sway the noble men then the rest of the citizens would follow suit, so he gave them time to consider their decision.

The emperor returned days later, and the seven men were resolute in their decision to remain Christian. The emperor sentenced them to death, and the seven men gave away all their goods to the poor and retired to the cave to pray and prepare for death. In the city, the remaining Christians were angry and revolted against the emperor's decision, so he knew he had to tread carefully with his decisions. He decided that the least contentious way to carry out the sentence was to brick up the cave as the men slept and let nature take its course.

News of the martyrs reached the city, and a group of Christians traveled to the site and wrote the names of the men and their story on the exterior of the cave.

Time passed, and the story of the noblemen was forgotten, and the empire returned to Christianity. One day a farmer was passing by the cave with his herd of cattle and decided that the cave would make a suitable cattle stall, so he unsealed the entrance and discovered the seven men asleep inside.

Once the seal was broken, all seven men awoke, and they believed they had been freed after just one night's sleep. One of the men decided to travel to the city and buy some breakfast for them all. He believed he was buying the last meal to enjoy before they gave themselves up and faced their death. When he arrived in the city and tried to buy food, he discovered his coins were out of date, and the buzz around the market was, "Who is this stranger, and why is he using such old coins?" The Christian Emperor Theodosius soon heard the rumors and assembled a group of Bishops and priests to investigate what was happening. They traveled to the cave and talked at length with the seven men, who realized that they had been asleep for 150 years and not just one night.

The identities of the men were established, and they died proclaiming their love for God and the truth of Christian beliefs. Theodosius immediately declared the cave a shrine and ordered that it be decorated with precious stones and gems. A church was erected at the site, and the emperor planned to build a golden tomb for the deceased martyrs until he had a dream where God told him to use the soil from the cave instead.

The event was hailed as a miracle, and there is a festival dedicated to the seven sleepers every year. The seven men were also declared saints by the Catholic Church, and the tale of their dedication has been reproduced throughout the world. Versions of the miracle appear in multiple cultures and would seem to indicate a modicum of truth behind the myth.

Chapter 6:

Alexander the Great

One of the greatest sons of Ephesus was Alexander the Great, one of the most influential figures in history. His masterful command and warfare tactics were legendary, and he remained unbeaten in battle before he died in 323 BC. The military genius was so influential that some of his military tactics are still used by armies across the world, including Iran and Pakistan.

Interesting Facts about Alexander the Great

1. He was born on the same night as the Temple of Artemis was burned in Ephesus. His father was Philip II of Macedonia, and his mother, Olympia, had a dream that a thunderbolt hit her stomach as she gave birth to Alexander. Some scholars and religious leaders of the time interpreted this to mean that Alexandria's real father was Zeus. Philip II was a great leader who defeated Athens and Thebes and established a Greek federation

known as the League of Corinth, of which he was the leader.

2. Philip II was the original battle genius. While it's true that Alexander was a military genius, his father gave him the best start in battle with an army of Macedonian fighting machines that was the most effective army of the time. When Philip took charge of the Macedonian forces, they were a rabble with little training and equipment; they could barely march together, let alone fight. Philip provided them with impressive weapons made from the natural resources available and taught them key moves in battle to ensure their success. Thanks to Philip's reforms, the army that Alexandria inherited was the greatest in the world.

3. He had a great teacher. Aristotle was the most celebrated philosopher in history, and hiring him as a teacher would normally be unthinkable, even for kings. However, when Alexander was young, Aristotle lost his home in Stagira to fire. Philip promised to rebuild and improve his home in exchange for his tutelage.

4. His father was assassinated. Macedonia had a reputation for assassinating those in power, and Philip was no different. He had left his first wife Olympia and her son behind and married again. In 336 BC, he attended a wedding feast for the daughter of his fourth wife and was killed by a member of his bodyguard team. He was stabbed in the ribs before his assassin took flight and was pursued by the other members of the team. The assassin was then stabbed until he died.

5. Alexander didn't automatically become King. Because of his lineage and his mother being from Epirus, Alexander was only half Macedonian, and his father had sired many potential heirs. Alexander had to murder a couple of wives and daughters along with two Macedonian princes on his bloody path to the throne. He also had to contend with several rebellious factions who were intent on keeping him from taking his rightful place as the King of Macedonia.

6. He married three times and only had one child. His father may have been a renowned lover of the ladies, but Alexander was a one-man woman. He fell in love with the daughter of a

Bactrian nobleman named Roxanne, and they married and had a son known as Alexander IV. After his death, she became close to Olympia, Alexander's mother, and the pair raised his child.

7. He nearly died at the site of his first battle. In 334 BC, Alexander crossed the Granicus River and encountered Persian forces waiting for him. The ensuing battle was so brutal and bloody he was nearly killed in the attack. Once he had won the hard-fought battle, Alexander slaughtered all the Greek mercenaries that had served with the Persian army to send a message to the world that Alexander would not allow treachery and those who opposed them would be dealt with harshly.

8. Despite the odds, he defeated Darius of Persia. Darius was one of the most successful Persian leaders, and his army outnumbered Alexander 100%. However, the Macedonian army was well-trained and equipped and was led by the most effective leader ever. He was defeated twice by Alexander, which effectively cost him his life and his dynasty. Alexander gained control of

Persia and Macedonia and fueled his ambitions to conquer other lands like India.

9. He was lucky. Alexander was saved from death multiple times, but the most famous intervention was by Cleatus the Black at the battle of Granicus River, who sliced off the arm of a Persian soldier who was just about to deal a lethal blow to Alexander. At other times his luck was still there but not as effective. He suffered multiple serious injuries and wounds during his short life. The worst injury he suffered was during the Indian campaign when his lung was punctured by an arrow.

10. He was dedicated to uniting his Greek and Persian subjects. In 324 BC, Alexander made a huge gesture to unite his warring citizens, and he organized a huge wedding ceremony where his high-ranking officers would marry Persian noblewomen in order to unify the two cultures. It is rumored that Alexander also took a wife but never consummated the union. Unfortunately, the rest of the weddings mostly ended in divorce just a short time later, so the whole exercise proved futile.

11. Alexander loved his wine. One of the most surprising facts about the great leader is his reputation for over-imbibing and getting into drunken brawls. There are two separate reports that at least two of his close friends were killed by his hand during these brawls, one of them being Cleatus the Black, who had previously saved his life in battle.

12. He died in 323 BC at the age of 32. Although Macedonian leaders were often assassinated, the cause of Alexander's death is unclear. He may have been assassinated, or he may have died from a series of effects from his wounds. Or his liver could have given up after being soaked in alcohol too many times. Official reports say he fell into a fever and was bedridden for a week before his death. What really happened is all down to conjecture.

13. His vast empire collapsed after his death. Due to his success, the empire he left behind consisted of an array of cultures and warring factions. He hadn't named a clear heir, and his son was too young to take command. This situation led to a war of succession that would see many try to

take command and fail. The war lasted forty years and was eventually settled by dividing the empire into three parts.

14. His tomb may not contain his remains. Ptolemy seized Alexander's body and returned it to Alexandria to lay in rest, but all records of where it is and what it contains disappeared at the end of the 4th century AD. The whereabouts remain a mystery, and there is some speculation that they may have been removed completely and lie elsewhere.

15. His legacy lives on. There are at least 16 cities around the world named after the great leader, and 10 of them are in the US. Across the globe, there are at least another 15 locations that aren't cities but are named Alexandria. His tactics and military strategies may never affect your life, but chances are you may travel to or meet someone whose birthplace or home is in Alexandria. This alone makes his story one of the greatest ever told and will remain in history for the rest of time.

Chapter 7:

What to Do in Ephesus

Now you have finished your sojourn through history and rubbed shoulders with some of the people who have passed through the city. You have learned their stories and got to know them and the surroundings they would have experienced. But what if you could visit Ephesus today? What would you see? Crowds of people just like in its heyday, but this time they would be tourists, and they are visiting to see the ruins of the ancient city rather than to shop in the agoras and trade slaves. If you are lucky enough to ever join them, here are some of the attractions waiting for you in the magnificent city of Ephesus.

What to Expect in Modern Ephesus

1. Wander around the City Center of Ephesus

The ancient city is waiting for you, and the walking trip around the main points takes around two hours. The entrance fee includes admission to some of the other areas, while some incur additional costs. The ancient city is open every day except for significant religious holidays between the hours of 8 am and 7 pm. The best time to visit is early in the morning or late in the afternoon.

2. The Ruins of the Celsus Library

In its day, this library was the third biggest in the ancient world and contained the tomb of its founder Tiberius Celsus. At the height of its popularity, it contained over 14 thousand scrolls, and huge reading rooms were specially designed to keep them safe from outside elements.

3. Visit the House of the Virgin Mary

We already know a lot about the Mother of God and her connection to Ephesus, but the house is a must-see part of your travels. It is customary when you enter the house to wear a scarf on your head to show respect for its sacred resident.

4. Imagine Yourself Watching a Show at the Ancient Theater

The ancient theater of Ephesus is a vast auditorium, and unlike some of the ruins, you get a real feel for what it felt like to sit in the 25-thousand-capacity theater and take your place on one of the 65 rows of seats. The stage may have collapsed, but the rows of seats are solid, and you can imagine crowds of people cheering on their favorite gladiator or joining in with the celebrations for the wine god Dionysus during the vine festivals.

The Ancient Theater is largely regarded as the home of drama, and its vast audiences would watch in wonder as actors took to the stage adorned in masks to represent humans and Gods as they fought epic battles and enacted myths from history. Over time, these performances developed into the contemporary theater we see today, and these masks became the forerunners of the popular laughing and crying masks that serve as an international symbol of the theater.

5. Explore the Temple of Hadrian

This Temple has only recently been excavated, so you can be one of the most recent people to view the magnificent friezes and artwork thought to have dated from 305 AD and were dedicated to Hadrian.

6. Visit the Prytaneion

If you are interested in how the government worked back in its heyday, then visit the Prytaneion and see where the city rulers would meet and sit by the fire of Hestia as they made important decisions. Governments were an important part of the city, and democracy was the very heart of how it worked. The mayor, or Pritan of Ephesus, was tasked with the important task of keeping the sacred fire alight. If it went out, it was believed the city would fall into disarray.

For those of you who want to have a night in the city, visit the official guesthouse at the Prytaneion.

7.   Pass through the Heracles Gate

The two pillars bear the relief of Heracles and are joined by an arch. There are two small motifs below the reliefs of the Nike symbol that dates the construction to around 400 AD.

8.   Stroll Down Harbor Street

Once you have seen the ancient theater take a leisurely walk down one of the most spacious streets of the ancient world, it is 528m long and 11m wide. Columns adorn the street, and you can find many interesting galleries and shops along the street. There is a highly sophisticated sewage system underneath the thoroughfare that wouldn't look out of place in some "modern" cities. It was named Harbor Street because the merchants and visiting dignitaries would be met here with ceremonies and plenty of pomp and pageantry. Close your eyes and imagine Kings and high-ranking government officials landing at Ephesus for the first time and experiencing this amazing sight.

9. Witness an Original Hammam

As you are in Turkey, you will already have seen hammams in the resort and all major cities, and they are more colloquially known as Turkish baths. The hammam at Ephesus is a bathhouse built by a wealthy individual named Skolastika for the citizens of the city to use. It was a place of relaxation and a social hub and could accommodate up to 1000 people at one time. There are 4 sections, the Caldarium, tepidarium, frigidarium, and apodyterium. The hot room was visited first, followed by the warm water room, before the bather entered the cold water room to cool down before the dressing room.

10. The Temple of Domitianus

Another must-see temple is the one dedicated to the emperor Domitian, which was the first time a Roman temple had been built in Ephesus. It was constructed in the 1st century AD and was huge and very ornate. However, as time went by, the Ephesians began to resent the cruelty and mismanagement that became synonymous with his rule, and they destroyed the Temple in anger. The foundations are the only remaining part of this once magnificent Temple but still worth a look.

11. See the Pollio Fountain

If you want to cool down, look at the fountain built as a mausoleum for the emperor Pollio by his stepson. Step inside and see the small pool constructed there as you imagine how bathing there would be a welcome relief from the heat. The water for the pool came from the well of the agora and illustrates how the different factions worked together.

12. Witness the Aqueducts of Ephesus

Marvel at the intact aqueducts that were built in the Byzantine era and are still viable today. The marble blocks are arranged into arches over 15m high and are impressive and functional. You can see the route the water took to distribute throughout the city and supply all the areas needed.

13. Visit Marble Street and the "Love House"

Marble Street is a magnificent marble-covered walkway and road that leads from the Ancient Theater to the Celsius Library. The people of Ephesus were among the first in the world to embrace urban culture and the need for people to travel freely throughout the city. Art and carvings were used to impress the populace rather than being kept in private homes. Just ahead of Marble Street is the world's first billboard with a picture of a woman's head and foot engraved in stone. This signaled the position of the "Love House" a popular calling place for sailors and weary travelers who had landed in the city. It is written that every man had to perform a ritual in front of the statue of Aphrodite before they were granted permission to enter the house.

14. Visit a Truly Public Toilet System That Will Make Your Eyes Water

What do you think of when you hear the phrase "public toilet?" The restroom at the garage or in a restaurant, perhaps? Or maybe the portable toilet at a festival or concert? Whatever preconception you have, be prepared to have your mind blown by the public toilets of Ephesus. While we expect privacy even in most public places when we go to the toilet, the Romans had other ideas.

We know the Romans were hygienic; the terrace houses had central heating and sanitation, but it seemed that when it came to public defecating, they had different rules.

Visit the public latrines at Ephesus, and the first thing you notice is the lack of walls. The latrines are made up of a row of seats with holes that lead to a flow of clean water underneath, and while the Romans sat and did their business, they openly chatted and were social with the people in the other seats. These toilets were free and seen as just as much of a social area as the local market.

15. Visit the Vedius Gymnasium

The gladiators were always training for combat, as were Roman soldiers. They needed a dedicated area to train, and in the 2nd century AD, a wealthy citizen built this magnificent center for cultural and sports education and improvement. A huge bath dominates the center of the gym, while a ceremonial room, training area, and stadium can be found on the outskirts.

16. Visit St. Johns Basilica

St. John was the trusted companion of the Virgin Mary, and a monumental tomb built in his honor was the second largest religious building Ephesus saw, the first being the Temple of Artemis. As Christianity grew and pilgrimages became popular, the basilica became a haven for Christians, and they have flocked there ever since the Middle Ages. Today you can experience the same journey and feel how special the basilica is, although you will have to pay an additional fee for the privilege.

17. See the Whole Area from the Top of Ayasuluk Hill

If you have the stamina to reach the top of the hill, you will be rewarded with a view that will take your breath away. From this vantage point, you can see the whole of Ephesus and the magnificent Oppression Gate guarding the city. You can pick out the baths, the castle, and the other structures while marveling at the city walls and their inner fortifications. This hill has been the subject of restoration since the 1960s and is a major part of the UNESCO pledge to keep the area as natural and rural as possible. It is considered one of the most important rural areas in Western Anatolia and has numerous resources that must be preserved and celebrated.

18. Refresh Your Energy at the Local Bakery

Walking around Ephesus can be exhausting, and at the end of the day, you deserve a treat, so visit the Efes Firin Café and Bakery for a refreshing cup of tea or coffee. They serve traditional versions of tea, or you can try a more local apple or mint tea. Treat yourself to a tasty pastry or baklava and enjoy the taste of Turkey. When you are feeling all refreshed and ready to leave the site, check out the souvenir shop for some impressive pieces to take back home with you.

Bottom line: Although a lot of the site is in ruins, you can still experience the smells and sounds of ancient Greece and the Roman era. Ephesus is an important part of world history, and you should revel in the chance to be part of that. The world is always changing, so it's a great way to step back into the past and try to imagine what it felt like to be part of the changing cultures of this once-influential city.

1

Conclusion

Now you have made your way through the streets of Ephesus and met the amazing people who once walked the same path, does it make you feel as if you are part of history? Do you feel like a citizen of the world and part of something so important it changed the world as we know it? That's what places like Ephesus do to you. They inspire you to learn more and be more appreciative of what happened in the past that has influenced your present life. They teach you to step outside of your own reality and gain a greater perspective on life. They teach you that, eventually, we are all consigned to history but that some people have made a bigger impression than most.

Hopefully, the book has made you eager to visit more historical sites or even Ephesus itself. Turkey is amazing, and the people will make you feel like family while the surroundings will take your breath away.

References

"20 Facts about Alexander the Great." History Hit, 2018, www.historyhit.com/facts-about-alexander-the-great/.

Admin. "Life in the Terrace Houses of Ephesus." Shutters & Sunflowers, 25 Oct. 2015, shuttersandsunflowers. com/life-in-the-terrace-houses-of-ephesus/.

AncientPages.com. "Fascinating Legend of the Seven Sleepers of Ephesus." Ancient Pages, 31 Oct. 2016, www. ancientpages.com/2016/10/31/fascinating-legend-of-the-seven-sleepers-of-ephesus/.

Ephesian, The. Famous People of Ephesus - All That You Need to Know Before Visiting Ephesus. 23 Nov. 2021, www.theephesus.com/famous-people-of-ephesus/.

"Ephesus Turkey - Private Tours, Excursions, Airport Transfers." Ephesus Turkey, www.ephesusturkey.com/ ephesus-highlights/commercial-agora/.

"Founding Myth of Ephesus." Ephesus, ephesus.us/mythology/founding-myth/.

Mark, Joshua. "Ephesus." World History Encyclopedia, 2 Sept. 2009, www.worldhistory.org/ephesos/.

Natalie. "Ephesus Ancient City: Ruins, Terrace Houses and Landmarks." Turkish Travel Blog, 21 June 2023, turkishtravelblog.com/ephesus-turkey-ancient-ruins-city/#Roman_City_Houses_on_the_Northern_Slopes.

"Seven Wonders of the World | List & Pictures." Encyclopædia Britannica, 2019, www.britannica.com/topic/Seven-Wonders-of-the-World.

Zeynep. "24 Things To-Do in Your Ephesus Trip." Turkey Things, 4 Nov. 2020, turkeythings.com/things-to-do-in-ephesus

www.ingramcontent.com/pod-product-compliance
Lightning Source LLC
Chambersburg PA
CBHW052223150726

48002CB00003B/1246